For more information about Cape Cod Eco-Tales, visit us online:
www.capecodecotales.com

Heathland Habitat

by Heidi Clemmer
illustrated by Marisa Picariello

A rustle in the **broom crowberry** catches the attention of Hannah the eastern hognose snake.

Slithering slowly alongside the low-growing shrubs scattered across the dunes, Hannah is not worried. She is nicely **camouflaged** in her yellow-brown skin which blends almost perfectly with the sandy soil of Cape Cod's **coastal heathlands**.

Just as Hannah is about to pounce on Willy the white-footed mouse, Rusty the red fox crosses her path. Hannah quickly rolls onto her back as hognose snakes do when they feel they are in danger, and "plays dead".

The fox sniffs at Hannah and turns away, suddenly disinterested in his **prey**.
This is just enough time for Willy to escape, as Hannah the hognose snake continues to hunt for her mid-day meal.

Vinny the vesper sparrow has been watching the excitement from his perch higher upon the grassy heathland **plains**. It is nearly twilight, and Vinny will soon begin defending his ground nest made of grass, weeds, and rootlets by singing his evening song; a slow series of 4 musical notes that sometimes sound like: "come-come-where-where-all-together-down-the-hill."

Meanwhile, Hannah's upland search has been a success!

A plump little toad (the favorite snack of an eastern hognose snake), is busy pursuing a dragonfly and is quickly snatched up by this very hungry **reptile**.

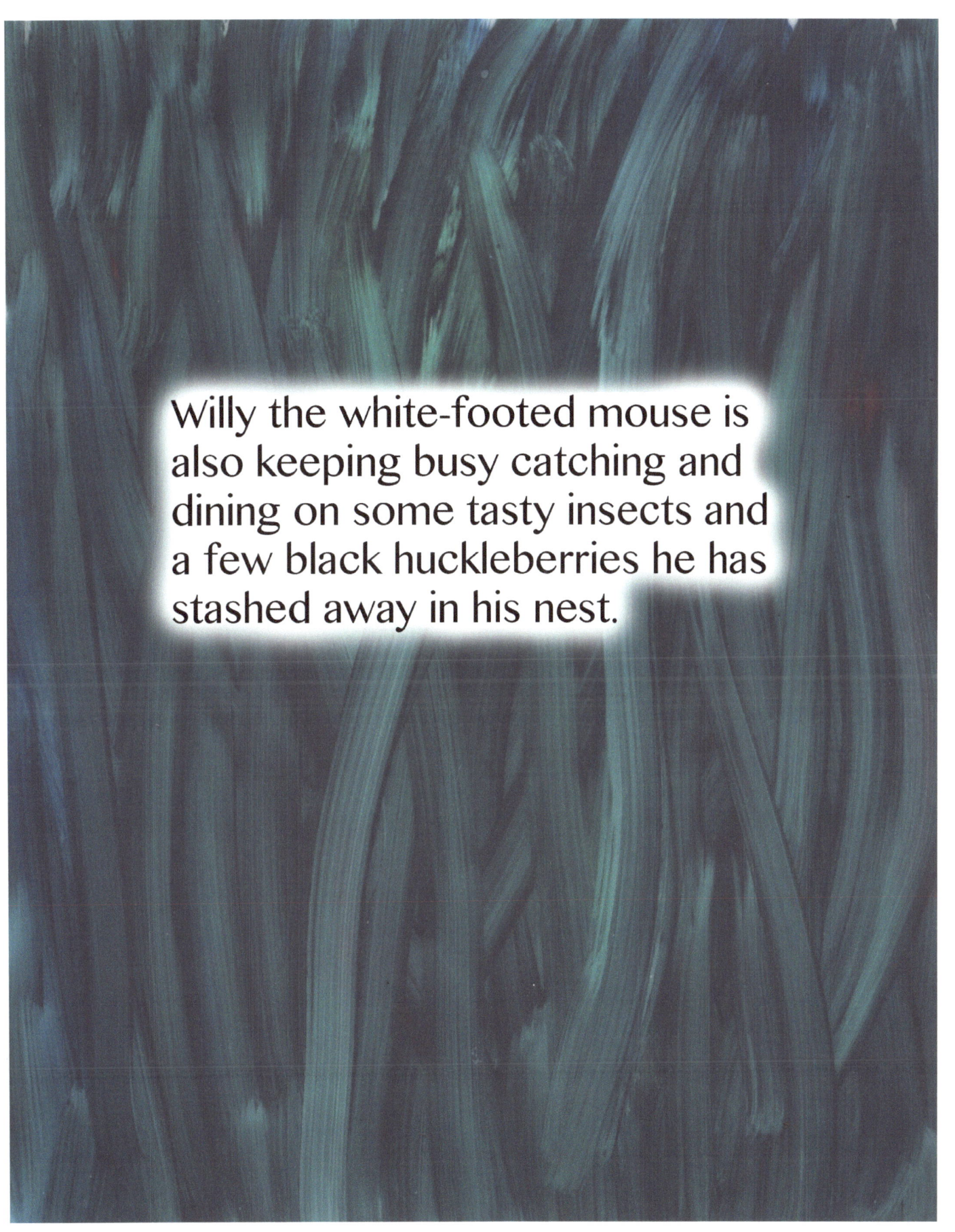

Willy the white-footed mouse is also keeping busy catching and dining on some tasty insects and a few black huckleberries he has stashed away in his nest.

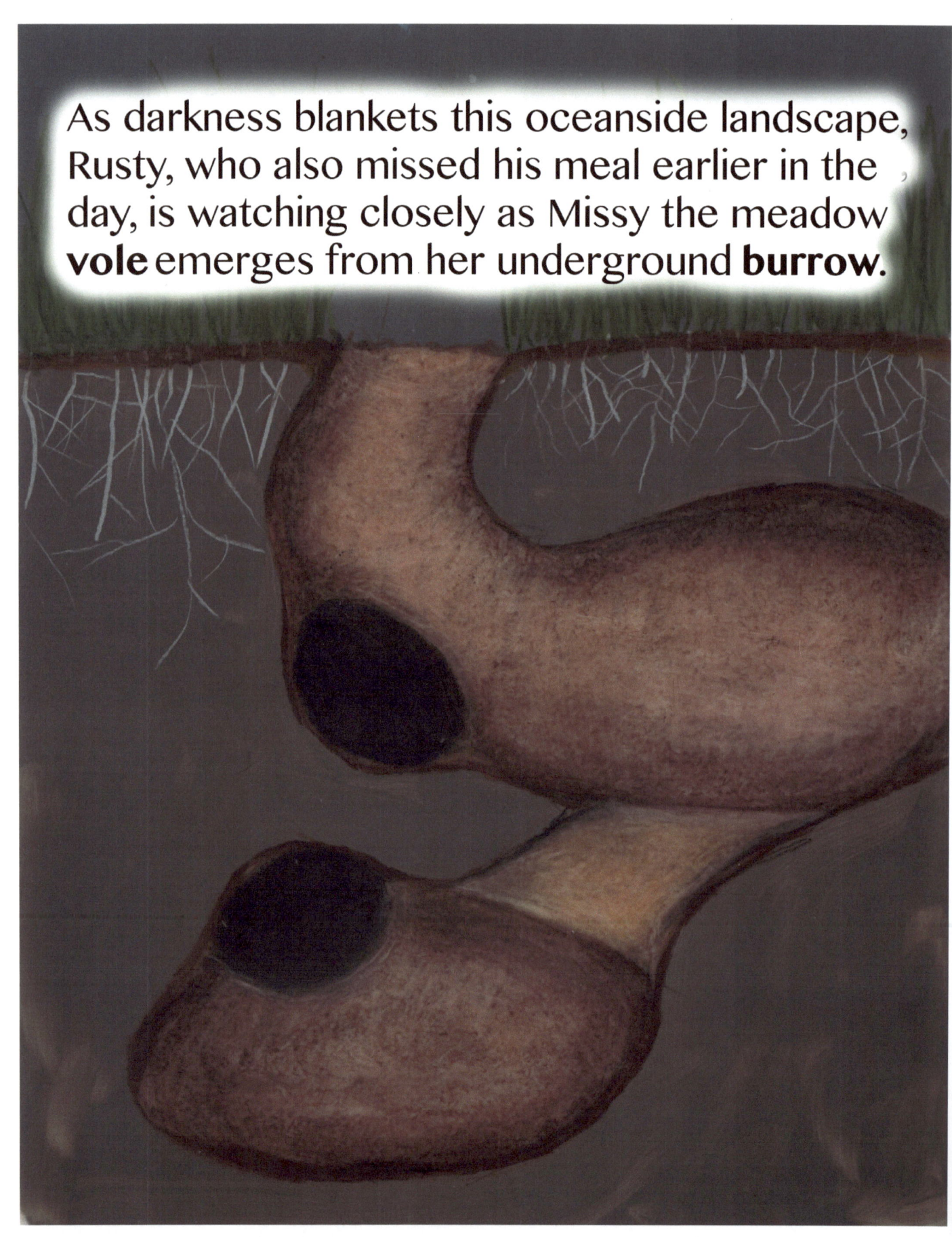

As darkness blankets this oceanside landscape, Rusty, who also missed his meal earlier in the day, is watching closely as Missy the meadow **vole** emerges from her underground **burrow**.

She is most active at night, running back and forth across the heathlands creating little paths throughout the thick grass, and digging extra "rooms" in her burrow to store food for the winter.

The fox begins to stalk the tiny **rodent**, but all of the little paths confuse him and Missy is able to dart into one of the burrows.

Not only is Missy saved, but so is a very important **eco-system**.

Missy is one of the many heathland creatures which keep their **habitat** healthy just by living in it!

A grass-eater, the little vole's "poops" are full of tiny seeds and other **nutrients**. The new plants they create cover the heathlands, providing shelter from weather, hiding places from **predators**, and plenty of material for the heathland dwellers to build nests which protect their young.

Lucky for Rusty, the red fox is able to quickly **adapt** to a new **environment**. As the sun rises above the ocean behind him, Rusty trots toward the nearby **scrub pine** forest, where he will surely find himself his long-awaited meal!

COASTAL HEATHLAND

Environmental Characteristics:

The heathlands of Cape Cod have adapted to the harsh seaside conditions with their thick mats of shrubs and low-lying bushes that hold back the sandy soil and help to prevent erosion. They are regularly lost to development.

Animal Life:
Eastern hognose Snake
Red Fox
White-footed Mouse
Meadow Vole
Vesper Sparrow

Plant Life:
Broom Crowberry
Beach Heather
Black Huckleberry

GLOSSARY

Adapt: to change something to suit a different environment

Broom Crowberry: a flowering plant that grows in dry, sandy soil

Burrow: a hole or tunnel dug by a small animal

Camouflaged: hidden or disguised to blend in with the environment

Coastal Heathlands: open areas of sand and shrubs along the coast

Eco-system: a "community" of interacting organisms and their environment

Environment: the surroundings in which a person, plant, or animal lives

Habitat: the natural home of an animal, plant, or other organisms

Nutrients: substances that provide nourishment for growth

Plain: a large area of flat land with few trees

Predator: an organism that lives by preying on other organisms

Reptile: a cold-blooded vertebrate
ex; snake, lizard, turtle

Rodent: a gnawing animal
ex; mouse, squirrel, hamster

Scrub pine: a type of pine tree with a scrubby growth; usually found in dry, sandy soil

Uplands: high or hilly landscapes

Vole: a small, mouse-like burrowing rodent

THE AUTHOR

Heidi Clemmer was an educator at Wellfleet Elementary School for 21 years. Cape Cod Eco-Tales is the result of her passion for enlightening her students and others to the varied and significant eco-systems that dominate the outer cape landscape.

THE ILLUSTRATOR

Marisa Picariello is a Wellfleet resident who studied art at Wheaton College. She finds inspiration in the natural world and has always enjoyed exploring the Cape Cod landscape.

www.ingramcontent.com/pod-product-compliance
Lightning Source LLC
Chambersburg PA
CBHW041829280526
45792CB00006B/2035